THE SPACES BETWEEN YOUR FINGERS

a parable

by Matthew Ross Smith
with illustrations by Dan Waldron

Have you ever really looked at the spaces between your fingers? Not the fingers themselves—the flesh and bones and joints and nails—the parts that make up the whole—but the spaces *b e t w e e n* them. You probably haven't. It's okay. Go ahead, look now. Not much there, huh? Just some empty spaces? Some empty air?

Well, that's what I used to think, too...

But that was before I started taking walks with my grandfather.

My grandfather was a famous man...well, he was famous for our little town. He'd been the town doctor for fifty years. Next time you're doing your chores and it seems like they're taking forever, just imagine how long fifty years is.

Back then, I couldn't imagine doing anything for fifty years. Not even playing baseball. Then again, I probably didn't love baseball as much as he loved being a doctor.

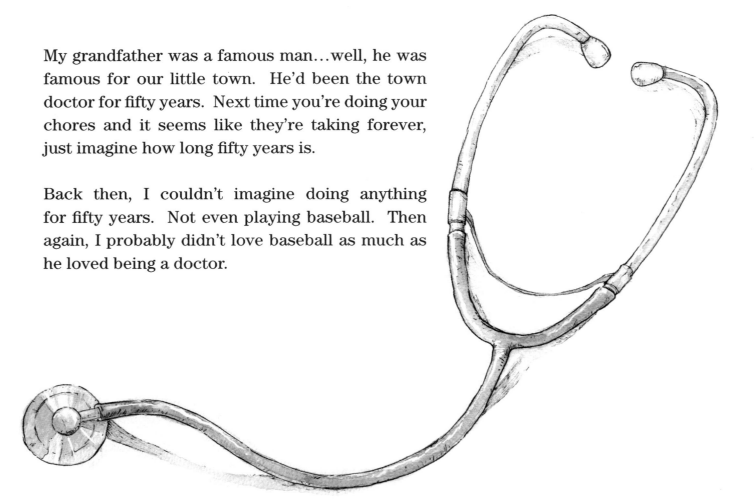

And when you truly love something, it's not like a chore at all.

I wasn't like all the other kids in my class. I wasn't afraid of things. I wasn't afraid of snakes. I wasn't afraid of spiders. I wasn't afraid of germs. I wasn't even afraid of the dark—not even when it closed in around me at night. I just waited until I got used to it, and it got used to me.

The only thing I didn't really like was being alone.

No matter how hard I tried, I couldn't get used to that.

My grandfather wasn't afraid of things, either. Before he became a doctor, he was a fighter pilot in the Second World War. He showed me his Presidential Medal and it said: "For exceptional bravery and valor."

When he told me stories I imagined that I was there with him in the cockpit, which was great, because the only thing better than looking up at the clouds...

... is looking down at them.

When we took walks, it seemed like there wasn't a person in the whole town my grandfather hadn't fixed.

"You fixed my leg!" a jogger said. "I never would've been able to run!"

"You fixed my hand!" a musician said. "I never would've been able to play!"

When people greeted my grandfather on the street, he always said two things. First he said: "You're very welcome." And then he said: "I want to introduce you to someone very special to me. This is my grandson, Matthew. We're on our way to feed the ducks."

In that way, I came to know everyone in the whole town.

And they loved me, because they loved him.

To get to the Duck Pond, we had to cross a very busy street. When he took my hand, our fingers interlocked like gears on a bike. **Therewasnospacebetweenthem.** His hands were big and strong, but still soft, which was why he must've been such a good doctor.

One day at The Pond we pressed our hands into some wet cement. Before it hardened a duck waddled through it, too—just because it was stupid, I thought. But my grandfather said it was in case he ever got lost he could always find his way back home, by following his footprints.

"How come his toes are stuck together like that?" I asked.

"Because it helps him glide through the water," he said.

My grandfather taught me lots of things like that, things that seem obvious now that I'm older.

One day, though, my grandfather didn't come for our walk.

"Where's Poppy?" I asked Mom.

"He's sick," she said. "He'll be back tomorrow."

She didn't say more but I could tell she was worried. She spent the whole night on the phone with her sisters, tangling the cord between her fingers.

I've never told anyone this…but the next week I found my grandfather doing something very strange. He was in his office, and all the books were strewn about the floor. It was a mess. He was standing on a chair, sweeping the carpet.

"What are you doing?" I asked.

"I opened up this book," he said, "and the craziest thing happened. All the words fell out onto the floor."

He'd swept the words into little piles.

"I keep hearing this voice," he said. "It's whispering:

I am the space
Between word and page.
Without me
*They would fall ap*ₐₚₐᵣₜ."

I listened real close, but I didn't hear a thing.

A few months later, I found him doing something even stranger.

He was in the bathroom, rubbing a glue stick all over the mirror.

"What are you doing?" I asked.

"I was shaving," he said, "and the craziest thing happened. My reflection fell right off the glass, into the sink."

He'd plugged up the sink, to keep it from going down. But he couldn't get it to stick again. "That same voice," he said. "It's haunting me:

I am the space
Between reflection
and mirror. Without me
They would fall apart."

I listened real close. But again, I didn't hear a thing.

My grandfather was changing.
When we met our friends now,
he couldn't remember their
names.   He only addressed
them after I did, and seemed
anxious to get away.

We still held hands when we
crossed the busy street, but
somehow it felt different. As
if I was leading him, instead of
the other way around.

And at The Duck Pond, he
didn't look at the ducks
anymore, but beyond them—
beyond the pond, beyond the
sunset, beyond everything.

"What's happening to Poppy?" I asked Mom.

"He's sick," she said again. "Only it's a different kind of sick. There's sickness of the body, like when you have a runny nose, or a rash. But then there's also sickness of the mind. That's much harder to treat because you can't see it, and a lot of times you can't even feel it."

"Is it contagious?"

"No. It's just something that some people get when they're old."

"So I'll get it?"

"No. By the time you're old, they'll already have the cure."

That explained why he couldn't just fix himself the way he'd always fixed everyone else. It was a disease of the mind, not the body.

But still…understanding didn't make it any easier. Mom said it would help if I read to him, so I did. I read him the same story every day after school, and every day he was surprised by the ending, as if he'd never heard it before.

He seemed at peace then, smiling back at me, listening, as if he'd finally found whatever he'd been searching for.

The day he died was the saddest day of my life. When my mother told me, I ran to the Duck Pond, alone, even though it was winter. I brushed away the snow and put my hand over the cement handprints we'd made, but my hand didn't fit anymore.

A few weeks later I felt a little better, but only because it was my birthday. My mother bought me a new mitt and a vanilla cake. She handed me a card and I thought it was another one from my aunts, but it wasn't. It was a letter from my grandfather.

Dear Matthew,

I wanted to write and thank you for reading to me all these weeks—I can't tell you how much it's meant to me. Your grandmother says you've been here every day. In fact, you're just leaving now. I'll have to write this letter before I forget all that I want to say.

Everyone thinks I'm sick—and maybe I am. But a part of me thinks I'm just beginning to see things in a new way. What makes the world so great is that there are so many different things in it. Take a field, for example. Stand in an empty field and all you might see is green grass for miles. But if you get down and look real close, you'll notice that every blade is a little different from the next.

In order for things to be different—for them to be special and unique—there must be spaces between them. A few months ago, or maybe it was years, something funny started happening with my eyes. They began to focus not on the things themselves, but on the spaces between them.

At first it was neat, but after a while it made me sad (and even a little scared) because if there were these spaces between everything—even between words and pages, reflections and mirrors—then how could two things ever really touch? They couldn't. There would always be a space, keeping them apart. Keeping them as parts, I mean. Just a bunch of parts. And when I looked at the world that way, as a whole bunch of parts, I began to feel lonely.

Lately, though, I'm feeling better. I still see the spaces, but what I've realized is that they exist for a reason, and it's not to keep us apart. It's the opposite. They're there to hold us together. Think how hard it would be to read this letter if the words kept falling from the page. But they don't. They stick. There's a force, holding them together.

And so it will be with you and me. Any time you want to find me, you don't have to look far. Just look down at the spaces between your fingers—where my hand used to be—and instead of thinking of all that's keeping us apart, remember this great force that's holding us together, and always will.

I'll see you again, but you have a long life to lead before then—fifty, sixty, seventy years! Imagine what you can do with all that time!

With love on your birthday,

And for all those to come,

I am,

Your Poppy

I confess that sometimes I still forget—we all do, it's inevitable, we forget. But every once in a while, when I'm riding in a car, and I stick my hand out the window into that great rushing current of air, I feel him there, and I remember.

I've grown up now, and I finally found something I love to do as much as he loved being a doctor: telling stories. I hope to do it for a long time. That's why I made this book, so that you could hear our story, and so that you might realize, as I did, that there's magic all around us, all the time...

...even in those tiny spaces between your fingers.

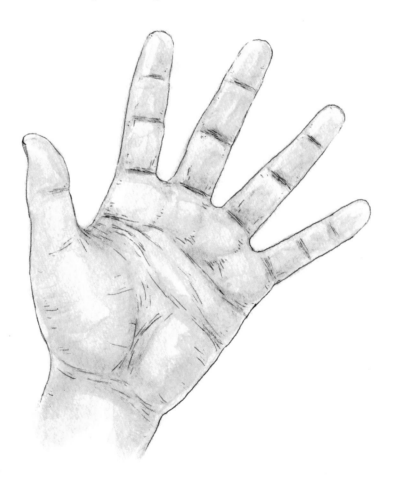

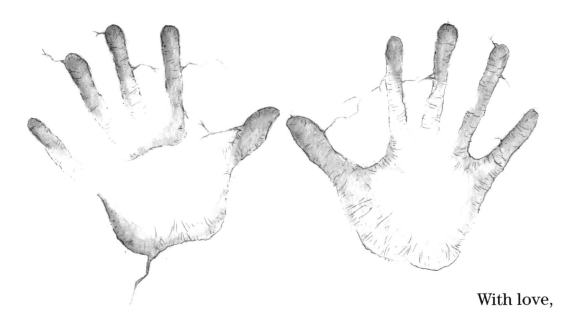

With love,

Matthew Ross Smith

In 2009, Matthew Ross Smith created
The Spaces Between Your Fingers Project
in memory of his grandfather.

100% of proceeds from this book were
used to support SBYF writing programs.

To learn more, please visit:

www.sbyfproject.com